KETO SN/

keto Smoothie Recipes. Many Irresistible Desserts to Lose Weight,
Detoxify, Fight Disease.

Table of Contents

Introduction.. 5

A Quick Overview of the Ketogenic Diet.................. 8

Avocado-Blueberry Smoothie 14

Energizing Smoothie...............................17

Green and Blue Smoothie..........................20

Blueberry Bliss 22

Berry Polka Dot Dance 25

Spinach Avocado Banana Smoothie 27

Almond Avocado Smoothie 29

Almond Strawberry Delight 32

Creamy Blackberry 34

Spicy Green Salad Smoothie..38

Superfood Coconut Smoothie 41

Dairy-Free Green Smoothie 43

Coconut Chai Smoothie 46

Spicy Green Salad Smoothie..48

Orange Chocolate Smoothie 51

Green Minty Protein Shake 54

Peppermint Patty 57

Kale, Spinach, and Strawberry Smoothie.............................62

Green Power Smoothie..64

Red Heart Smoothie..67

Orange-Carrot Smoothie 70

Superfood Smoothie 75

Silken Tofu Smoothie 78

Carrot and Leafy Green Smoothie.......................................80

Mango-Carrot Green Tea Smoothies 82

Creamy Chocolate Milkshake..85

Espresso Smoothie 88

Hazelnut Keto Coffee Smoothie..92

The Peanut Milkshake 95

The Keto Frapp..97

Rich n' Creamy Blackberry Smoothie...101

Cinnamon Roll Smoothie...105

Yummy Strawberry-Cheesecake Smoothie 107

Mango Berry Slush..110

Raspberry Cheesecake Blend...112

Strawberry-Almond Crunch Smoothie 114

Peach Pie Shake 118

Buttered Pumpkin Pie Coffee..120

Chocolate-Cayenne Shake..122

Peanut Butter Crunch Chocolate Smoothie 126

Whipped Chocolate Shake 128

Mango Almond Smoothie 131

Almond Strawberry Smoothie...133

Chocolate Avocado Cream Smoothie 136

Very Berry Strawberry Smoothie 138

Peach Coconut Smoothie 141

Coconut-Strawberry Smoothie 143

Cocoa-Coconut-Macadamia Smoothie..146

Chocolate-Coconut Tofu Smoothie 148

Almond Chocolate Blueberry Smoothie 151

Just Peachy Smoothies 153

Apricot Smoothie..156

Apricot Peachy Slush 158

Conclusion...161

3

Introduction

For years we were told that fats are bad for us and to be healthy we should eat more carbs. But as our knowledge of science and nutrition advanced, we now know fats aren't as bad as we once thought! This is where the Ketogenic Diet comes in. Scientific studies now show the dangers and risks associated with simple carb diets. At the same time many there are many studies that show the health benefits of a high fat low carb diet, including:

- **Increased Energy and Focus**

- **Increased Weight Loss**

- **Lowered Blood Sugar Levels**

- **Decrease in Hunger**

- **Lowered Bad Cholesterol Levels**

- **Reduction in Acne and Skin Inflammation**

One of the biggest challenges I face while on the Ketogenic Diet is snacking between meals. This is especially true when first starting out! Before our bodies start using fat as its main source of energy, our hunger levels are at its highest. That's why it's important to have healthy alternatives to our usual unhealthy impulses.

The Ketogenic friendly smoothies in this book are all quick and easy to make. You can drink them right away, or store them some place cold to have while you're at work. Either way, they will help keep you full until your next meal.

The book is divided into two sections. The first half is filled with nutrient dense drinks that's designed to give your body a jolt of vitamins and minerals. The other half consists of tasty keto-friendly snack drinks. Think of these drinks as little treats to congratulate yourself for sticking to the diet!

Thank you for reading the book, if you have any questions or comment I would love to hear them!

A Quick Overview of the Ketogenic Diet

Have you ever wanted to have more energy in your day, feel better and look better? Many people have found a way to achieve a better life with a simple diet. I know, it sounds too good to be true. Yet, it is really possible to gain more energy, feel better and look better by changing the way you eat. There is no magic pill, rather it is as simple as developing an eating plan that gives your body the nutrients it needs.

What is this magic eating plan? It is known as a Ketogenic Diet. This method of eating is not so new and has been around for thousands of years. Unfortunately, modern society is selecting convenience foods generally loaded with carbohydrates and refined sugars. Today, eating is often done on the run.

Convenience is what sells and manufacturers satisfy consumers' demands. These convenience foods come with preservatives, dyes, added refined sugar, salt and processed grains. While it may be convenient to our schedule, these foods are not convenient for our body to process.

The Ketogenic Diet may sound complex and technical; but simply put, this diet is feeding your body foods that it can process more easily. The human body is made to function using food for fuel, which in turn gives us energy. The Ketogenic Diet optimizes this process with the result of giving us more energy. There are four sources of fuel for the body: carbohydrates, fat, protein and ketones.

But what are ketones? Ketones occur when fat in the body is broken down. The result of a Ketogenic Diet is that fat and ketones become the main source of fuel for the body. The key to eating a Ketogenic Diet is to consume more fats, some protein and little carbohydrates. This allows the body to be in a state of nutritional ketosis.

Before starting any diet, you need to discuss the benefits/risks with your doctor. It is important to understand the impact a diet may have on your body and your medical conditions. This will help you choose a diet that will be safe and give optimal results.

Eating a Ketogenic Diet is not just eating a low carbohydrate diet. Rather than counting carbohydrates, consider being aware of your body and how it is responding to the foods you consume. Are you giving yourself the nutrients that you need? A Ketogenic Diet is a change in both lifestyle and mindset.

When the body uses carbohydrates to convert glucose to energy, blood sugar levels can drop fast. The results are hunger and cravings for sugar and carbohydrates. On a Ketogenic Diet, drops in blood sugar are minimized. This is because fats and ketones serve as fuel rather than quick burning carbohydrates.

Weight loss is hindered by foods that cause cravings for sugar, salt and fats. These addictive foods cause over consumption of food that never give a true feeling of satisfaction. Most often, processed foods are the culprits. On a Ketogenic Diet, these foods can be avoided and so are the resulting junk food cravings and hunger. Instead of calorie counting, stick to foods found in nature and that are simple to pronounce.

Foods such as grains, dairy and refined sugar cause inflammation in the body. Inflammation hinders weight loss and causes toxins to build up in your body. After starting the Ketogenic Diet, the toxins will be removed and inflammation will decrease.

The above is an over view of the Ketogenic Diet. If you would like to learn more I have a beginner's guide to the Ketogenic Diet where we go more in-depth with the mechanics of the diet and give you proven strategies to help you lose weight for good!

You will also learn...

- How to live a Ketogenic lifestyle
- Awesome Tips To Help You Stay On Track
- Over 40 Easy Recipes For All Meals - Breakfast, Lunch, Dinner and Snacks
- Macro and Micro Nutritional Information For Each Recipe!

Heavenly Nutritious Smoothies

These recipes are nutrient dense concoctions that will fill you up and keep you going throughout the day. These shakes are not only good for you but taste great too!

Avocado-Blueberry Smoothie

This smoothie is not green so even kids will love it. The avocado makes the consistency of the smoothie creamier and richer. The blueberries pack it with fiber and antioxidant, which helps fight off free radicals and heart disease.. I find that even without the added sweetener, the blueberries sweeten the smoothie enough.

Serves: 2
Prep. Time: 3 minutes
Blend Time: 2 minutes

Nutritional Facts

Serving Size: 219 g

Calories: 226

Total Fat: 14.4 g

Saturated Fat: 3.9 g   **Trans. Fat:** 0 g

Cholesterol: 10 mg

Sodium: 123 mg

Potassium: 361 mg

Total Carbohydrates: 12 g

Dietary Fiber: 4.3 g   **Sugar:** 6.1 g

Protein: 13.7 g

Vitamin A: 4%   **Vitamin C:** 13%

Calcium: 17%   **Iron:** 6%

Ingredients:

- 1/4 cup frozen blueberries, unsweetened
- 1/2 avocado, peeled, pitted, sliced
- 1 cup unsweetened almond milk, vanilla
- 1 scoop vanilla isolate protein or 2 tablespoons gelatin
- 1 tablespoon heavy cream
- 1 pack Stevia or 2 teaspoons Splenda

Directions :

1.   Put everything in a blender. Blend for until smooth. Pour in a glass. Enjoy!

****

Energizing Smoothie

Not only is this thick smoothie delicious, the cranberries pack it with anti-bacterial properties that help prevent kidney ulcers. Cranberry juice is also known to help prevent kidney and urinary tract infections. Recent studies also show that cranberries help reduce bad cholesterol (LDL) and increases the level of good cholesterol (HDL).

Serves: 2
Prep. Time: 3 minutes
Blend Time: 2 minutes

Nutritional Facts

Serving Size: 223 g

Calories: 192
Total Fat: 8.4 g
Saturated Fat: 1 g   **Trans. Fat:** 0 g
Cholesterol: 0 mg
Sodium: 33 mg
Potassium: 130 mg
Total Carbohydrates: 13.7 g
Dietary Fiber: 3.5 g   **Sugar:** 9.2 g
Protein: 13.2 g
Vitamin A: 0%   **Vitamin C:** 29%
Calcium: 2%   **Iron:** 9%

Ingredients:

- 1 cup berries, frozen
- 1 cup water
- 2 teaspoons Splenda or 1 packet Stevia
- 1 scoop vanilla whey isolate powder or 2 tablespoons gelatin plus 1 teaspoon vanilla extract
- 1 tablespoon flaxseed oil
- 1 tablespoon ground flaxseed
- 1 teaspoon unsweetened cranberry juice
- 2 teaspoons lemon juice
- 8 ice cubes

Directions :

1.   Put everything in a blender except the ice cubes. Blend for until smooth. Add in the ice cubes. Blend again. Pour in a glass. Enjoy!

****

Green and Blue Smoothie

Whenever I want to add greens into my smoothie, spinach is definitely my favorite green. It is not as bitter as other greens, such as kale, and they blend easy to create delicious smoothies. Blueberries and spinach also combine to make a smoothie that's packed with Vitamin K, which is important in bone health maintenance, and also rich in vitamin A, folate, manganese, iron, and magnesium.

Serves: 1
Prep. Time: 3 minutes
Blend Time: 2 minutes

Nutritional Facts

Serving Size: 382 g

Calories: 229
Total Fat: 4 g
Saturated Fat: 2 g   **Trans. Fat:** 0 g
Cholesterol: 6 mg
Sodium: 182 mg
Potassium: 440mg
Total Carbohydrates: 12.1 g
Dietary Fiber: 1.9 g   **Sugar:** 8.8 g
Protein: 38 g
Vitamin A: 57%   **Vitamin C:** 24%
Calcium: 27%   **Iron:** 10%

Ingredients:

- 1/4 cup frozen blueberries
- 1/3 cup unsweetened almond milk
- 1/2 cup Greek or Fage yogurt (plain or full-fat)

- 1 scoop vanilla isolate protein or 2 tablespoons gelatin plus 1 teaspoon vanilla extract
- 1 cup spinach, loosely packed
- 1/3 cup ice

Directions :

1.   Put everything in a blender except the ice cubes. Blend for until smooth. Add in the ice cubes. Blend again. Pour in a glass. Enjoy!

****

Blueberry Bliss

This simple low carb smoothie is both nutritious and delicious. Aside from the sweet taste, blueberries are considered as a superfood because its high antioxidant content.. Numerous studies also show that blueberries help lower blood pressure and contain anti-diabetic effects. Like cranberries, blueberries also have anti-bacterial properties.

Serves: 2
Prep. Time: 3 minutes
Blend Time: 2 minutes

Nutritional Facts

Serving Size: 320 g

Calories: 309
Total Fat: 24.2 g
Saturated Fat: 13.3 g   **Trans. Fat:** 0 g
Cholesterol: 78 mg
Sodium: 212 mg

Potassium: 231 mg

Total Carbohydrates: 10 g

Dietary Fiber: 1.4 g   **Sugar:** 5.6 g

Protein: 14.2 g

Vitamin A: 17%   **Vitamin C:** 5%

Calcium: 32%   **Iron:** 6%

Ingredients:

- 1/4 cup frozen blueberries, unsweetened
- 1 packet stevia or 2 teaspoons Splenda
- 1 scoop vanilla isolate protein or 2 tablespoons gelatin plus

1 teaspoon vanilla extract

- 16 ounces unsweetened almond milk, vanilla
- 4 ounces heavy cream

Directions :

1.   Put everything in a blender. Blend for until smooth. Pour in a glass. Enjoy!

Berry Polka Dot Dance

This smoothie will satisfy your sweet tooth with only 4.9 grams of net carbs. The flaxseeds pack the smoothie with dietary fiber, micronutrients, vitamin B1, manganese, and heart-friendly essential fatty acid omega 3.

Serves: 2
Prep. Time: 3 minutes
Blend Time: 2 minutes

Nutritional Facts

Serving Size: 268 g

Calories: 123
Total Fat: 4 g
Saturated Fat: 0 g   **Trans. Fat:** 0 g
Cholesterol: 0 mg
Sodium: 176 mg
Potassium: 314 mg
Total Carbohydrates: 8.8 g
Dietary Fiber: 3.9 g   **Sugar:** 3.7 g
Protein: 14.3 g
Vitamin A: 29%   **Vitamin C:** 22%
Calcium: 26%   **Iron:** 14%

Ingredients:

- 1 1/2 cup unsweetened almond milk
- 1 cup spinach
- 2 tablespoons flax seeds
- 1/3 cup frozen blackberries
- 1/3 cup frozen blueberries
- 1 scoop vanilla isolate protein or 2 tablespoons gelatin plus
1 teaspoon vanilla extract

Directions :

1.   Put everything in a blender. Blend for until
smooth. Pour into 2 glasses. Enjoy!

****

26

Spinach Avocado Banana Smoothie

This quick to make a delicious smoothie can be enjoyed as a breakfast or snack drink. With only a few ingredients, this smoothie is packed with nutrients that will give you the boost you need in the morning.

Serves: 5
Prep. Time: 3 minutes
Blend Time: 2 minutes

Nutritional Facts
Serving Size: 296 g

Calories: 197

Total Fat: 8 g

Saturated Fat: 1.7 g   Trans. Fat: 0 g

Cholesterol: 0 mg

Sodium: 62 mg

Potassium: 367 mg

Total Carbohydrates: 13.6 g

Dietary Fiber: 3.7 g   Sugar: 7 g

Protein: 20.6 g

Vitamin A: 24%   Vitamin C: 16%

Calcium: 4%   Iron: 5%

Ingredients:

- 2 cups spinach
- 1 large banana, frozen
- 1 avocado
- 1 tablespoon honey
- 1 pack gelatin or 1 scoop isolate protein
- 1 cup water
- 3 cups ice

Directions :

1.   Put all of the ingredients into the blender. Blend until smooth.

Almond Avocado Smoothie

The key to this smoothie is choosing a good almond butter. You will get most of your flavor from the almond butter you pick. Almond butter contains copper and calcium, both of which play a vital role in maintaining a healthy nervous system and healthy brain cells. Almond butter is also rich in vitamin E, magnesium, fiber, and healthy unsaturated fatty acids.

Serves: 2

Prep. Time: 3 minutes

Blend Time: 2 minutes

Nutritional Facts

Serving Size: 214 g

Calories: 359

Total Fat: 22.2 g

Saturated Fat: 6.9 g   **Trans. Fat:** 0 g

Cholesterol: 22 mg

Sodium: 128 mg

Potassium: 437 mg

Total Carbohydrates: 13.1 g

Dietary Fiber: 4 g   **Sugar:** 4.5 g

Protein: 28.7 g

Vitamin A: 6%   **Vitamin C:** 9%

Calcium: 18%   **Iron:** 6%

Ingredients:

- 1/2 avocado, peeled, pitted, sliced
- 1/2 cup half and half
- 1/2 cup unsweetened almond milk, vanilla
- 1/2 teaspoon vanilla extract
- 2 scoops vanilla isolate protein
- 1 tablespoons almond butter
- Pinch of cinnamon

- 1 packet stevia or 2 teaspoons Splenda
- 2-4 ice cubes

Directions :

1.   Put everything in a blender except the ice cubes. Blend for until smooth.
2.   Add in ice cubes. Blend again.
3.   Pour in a glass. Enjoy!

****

Almond Strawberry Delight

This refreshing smoothie is nutty with a creamy sweet taste. Aside from antioxidants, strawberries also potassium, folate, dietary fiber, manganese. Some of the health benefits include eye improvement and relief from arthritis, gout, high blood pressure, and various other cardiovascular related diseases.

Serves: 2

Prep. Time: 3 minutes

Blend Time: 2 minutes

Nutritional Facts

Serving Size: 334 g

Calories: 352

Total Fat: 24.2 g

Saturated Fat: 13.3 g   **Trans. Fat:** 0 g

Cholesterol: 78 mg

Sodium: 240 mg

Potassium: 219 mg

Total Carbohydrates: 9 g

Dietary Fiber: 1.3 g   **Sugar:** 5.2 g

Protein: 26 g

Vitamin A: 17%   **Vitamin C:** 12%

Calcium: 33%   **Iron:** 6%

Ingredients:

- 16 ounces unsweetened almond milk, vanilla
- 1 packet stevia or 2 teaspoons Splenda
- 4 ounce heavy cream
- 2 scoops vanilla isolate protein or 4 tablespoons gelatin plus 1 teaspoon vanilla extract
- 1/4 cup frozen strawberries, unsweetened

33

Directions :

1.   Put everything in a blender. Blend for until smooth.
        Pour in a glass. Enjoy!

****

Creamy Blackberry

This drink delicious smoothie is packed with anthocyanins, which are compounds that help keep the heart healthy. The fiber and magnesium of blackberries also promotes strong blood flow and prevents blockage in the arteries, which reduces the risk of strokes and heart attacks..

Serves: 2

Prep. Time: 3 minutes

Blend Time: 2 minutes

Nutritional Facts

Serving Size: 268 g

Calories: 300

Total Fat17 g

Saturated Fat: 10.4 g   Trans. Fat: 0 g

Cholesterol:62 mg

Sodium: 76 mg

Potassium: 156 mg

Total Carbohydrates: 12.2 g

Dietary Fiber: 3.8 g   Sugar: 7.6 g

Protein: 25.9 g

Vitamin A: 16%   Vitamin C: 26%

Calcium: 7%   Iron: 4%

Ingredients:

- 1 cup fresh blackberries
- 1 packet stevia or 2 teaspoons Splenda
- 3/4 cup heavy whipping cream
- 2 scoops vanilla isolate protein or 4 tablespoons gelatin plus
2 teaspoon vanilla extract
- 1 cup ice cubes

Directions :

1.   Put everything in a blender except the ice cubes.
    Blend for until smooth.
2.   Add in ice cubes. Blend again.
3.   Pour in a glass. Enjoy!

****

Spicy Green Salad Smoothie

When you can't eat your salad, drink one! The main component of this smoothie is white cabbage which is high in anthocyanins and vitamin K Cabbage is also high in vitamin C, which helps detoxify the body and remove toxins.

Serves: 2

Prep. Time: 3 minutes

Blend Time: 2 minutes

Nutritional Facts

Serving Size: 267 g

Calories: 51

Total Fat: 0.6 g

Saturated Fat: 0 g   **Trans. Fat:** 0 g

Cholesterol: 0 mg

Sodium: 33 mg

Potassium: 470 mg

Total Carbohydrates: 10.4 g

Dietary Fiber: 2.6 g   **Sugar:** 4.4 g

Protein: 2.6 g

Vitamin A: 81%   **Vitamin C:** 153%

Calcium: 7%   **Iron:** 13%

Ingredients:

- 1 cup fresh white cabbage
- 1 handful fresh baby kale
- 1 handful fresh parsley
- 1 lemon juice, squeezed into the blender
- 1 medium Roma or Heirloom tomato
- 1/2 cup water
- 1/2 habanero pepper, remove seeds
- 1/2 Italian cucumber
- 5–6 ice cubes

Optional:

- 1–2 tablespoon sunflower seeds
- Dash of cayenne pepper

Directions :

4.   Put everything in a blender except the ice cubes. Blend for until smooth.
5.   Add in the ice cubes. Blend again.
6.   Pour in a glass. Enjoy!

****

Superfood Coconut Smoothie

If love coconut cream in your dessert, then you will love coconut cream in your smoothie. Coconut cream, like coconut oil, is high antimicrobial compounds, which effectively fights viruses that cause measles, herpes, hepatitis, and the flu. The fatty acids in coconut cream are fat-burning saturated fat, which in itself is a natural antioxidant that helps fight free radicals. Moreover, coconut cream is cholesterol-free. Combined with blueberries, this smoothie is very creamy and super healthy.

Serves: 2

Prep. Time: 3 minutes

Blend Time: 2 minutes

Nutritional Facts

Serving Size: 173 g

Calories: 216

Total Fat: 15.3 g

Saturated Fat: 12.8 g   **Trans. Fat:** 0 g

Cholesterol: 0 mg

Sodium: 82 mg

Potassium: 235 mg

Total Carbohydrates: 9.1 g

Dietary Fiber: 2.5 g   **Sugar:** 5.6 g

Protein: 13.9 g

Vitamin A: 0%   **Vitamin C:** 12%

Calcium: 9%   **Iron:** 10%

Ingredients:

- 1/2 cup coconut cream
- 1/2 cup frozen blueberries, unsweetened
- 1/2 cup unsweetened almond milk, vanilla
- 1 scoop vanilla isolate protein or 2 tablespoons gelatin plus
1 teaspoon vanilla extract
- 2-4 ice cubes

Directions :

1. Put everything in a blender except the ice cubes. Blend for until smooth.
2. Add in ice cubes. Blend again.
3. Pour in a glass. Enjoy!

Dairy-Free Green Smoothie

Don't fret, the pineapple and the fruits in this smoothie cut right through the greens. With the pineapple, this smoothie can help cure coughs, aid weight loss, strengthen bones, and reduce inflammation, Pineapple is also an excellent source of manganese and vitamin C.

Serves: 6

Prep Time: 5 minutes

Blend Time: 2 minutes

Nutritional Facts

Serving Size: 229 g

Calories: 63

Total Fat: 3.5 g

Saturated Fat: 0.7 g   **Trans. Fat:** 0 g

Cholesterol: 0 mg

Sodium: 8 mg

Potassium: 196 mg

Total Carbohydrates: 8.4 g

Dietary Fiber: 2 g   **Sugar:** 4.7 g

Protein: 0.8 g

Vitamin A: 3%   **Vitamin C:** 37%

Calcium: 2%   **Iron:** 4%

Ingredients:

- 1 cup raw cucumber, peeled and sliced
- 1 cup romaine lettuce
- 1 tablespoon fresh ginger, peeled and chopped
- 1/2 cup kiwi fruit, peeled and chopped
- 1/2 Half avocado (remove pit and scoop flesh out of shell)

- 1/3 cup chopped fresh pineapple
- 2 tablespoons fresh parsley
- 3 teaspoons Splenda
- 4 cups water

Directions:

1.   Put everything in a blender Blend for until smooth. Enjoy!

Coconut Chai Smoothie

This smoothie is packed with anti-inflammatory, digestive, and antioxidant properties. The almond butter adds richness and a protein kick, while the flaxseeds add fiber and omega 3. Cinnamon helps reduce fatigue, increase circulation, and increase vitality. Finally, ginger stimulates the immune and the circulatory system.

Serves: 2
Prep. Time: 3 minutes
Blend Time: 2 minutes

Nutritional Facts

Serving Size: 148 g

Calories: 421
Total Fat: 38.8 g
Saturated Fat: 26.4 g   **Trans. Fat:** 0 g
Cholesterol: 0 mg
Sodium: 20 mg
Potassium: 493 mg
Total Carbohydrates: 13 g
Dietary Fiber: 4.9 g   **Sugar:** 4.9 g
Protein: 6.9 g
Vitamin A: 0%   **Vitamin C:** 6%
Calcium: 8%   **Iron:** 21%

Ingredients:

- 1/4 cup unsweetened shredded coconut
- 1 cup unsweetened coconut milk
- 1 tablespoon ground flaxseed
- 1 tablespoon pure vanilla extract
- 1 teaspoon ground cinnamon
- 1 teaspoon ground ginger
- 2 tablespoons almond butter
- Pinch of allspice
- 5 ice cubes

Directions:

1. Put everything in a blender except the ice cubes. Blend for until smooth.
2. Add in ice cubes. Blend again.
3. Pour in a glass. Enjoy!

****

Spicy Green Salad Smoothie

Spice up your day with this spicy smoothie. If you like it hot, you'll love this nutritious smoothie that's packed with vitamins and nutrients.

Serves: 2
Prep. Time: 3 minutes
Blend Time: 2 minutes

Nutritional Facts

Serving Size: 267 g

Calories: 51
Total Fat: 0.6 g
Saturated Fat: 0 g   **Trans. Fat:** 0 g
Cholesterol: 0 mg
Sodium: 33 mg
Potassium: 470 mg
Total Carbohydrates: 10.4 g
Dietary Fiber: 2.6 g   **Sugar:** 4.4 g
Protein: 2.6 g
Vitamin A: 81%   **Vitamin C:** 153%
Calcium: 7%   **Iron:** 13%

Ingredients:

- 1 cup fresh white cabbage
- 1 handful fresh baby kale
- 1 handful fresh parsley
- 1 lemon juice, squeezed into the blender
- 1 medium Roma or Heirloom tomato

49

- 1/2 cup water
- 1/2 habanero pepper, remove seeds
- 1/2 Italian cucumber
- 5–6 ice cubes

Optional:

- 1–2 tablespoon sunflower seeds
- Dash of cayenne pepper

Directions :

1. Put everything in a blender except the ice cubes. Blend for until smooth.
2. Add in the ice cubes. Blend again.
3. Pour in a glass. Enjoy!

****

50

Orange Chocolate Smoothie

This smoothie is a delicious orange-chocolate delight. You won't even guess that it's packed with spinach. The orange extract also helps your body absorb the iron in spinach.

Serves: 1

Prep. Time: 3 minutes

Blend Time: 2 minutes

<u>Nutritional Facts</u>

Serving Size: 304 g

Calories: 164

Total Fat: 5.1 g

Saturated Fat: 1.2 g   **Trans. Fat:** 0 g

Cholesterol: 0 mg

Sodium: 249 mg

Potassium: 444 mg

Total Carbohydrates: 8.5 g

Dietary Fiber: 4.9 g   **Sugar:** 0 g

Protein: 27.5 g

Vitamin A: 28%   **Vitamin C:** 7%

Calcium: 34%   **Iron:** 16%

Ingredients:

- 1/8 teaspoon orange extract
- 1 cup unsweetened almond milk
- 1 scoop chocolate or vanilla isolate protein
- 1/2 cup spinach
- 2 tablespoons unsweetened cocoa powder

Directions :

1.   Put everything in a blender except the ice cubes.
     Blend for until smooth.
2.   Add in ice cubes. Blend again.
3.   Pour in a glass. Enjoy!

****

Green Minty Protein Shake

Who didn't love chocolate chip ice cream as a kid? This satisfying smoothie will surely cure your sweet tooth.. It's so yummy, you won't even taste the greens. Great for kids too.

Serves: 2

Prep Time: 3 minutes

Blend Time: 2 minutes

Nutritional Facts

Serving Size: 265 g

Calories: 184

Total Fat: 10.8 g

Saturated Fat: 2.2 g   **Trans. Fat:** 0 g

Cholesterol: 0 mg

Sodium: 91 mg

Potassium: 379 mg

Total Carbohydrates: 9.4 g

Dietary Fiber: 4 g   **Sugar:** 4.4 g

Protein: 13.6 g

Vitamin A: 30%   **Vitamin C:** 15%

Calcium: 11%   **Iron:** 6%

Ingredients:

- 1 packet stevia or 2 teaspoons Splenda
- 1/4 teaspoon peppermint extract
- 1/2 cup almond milk, unsweetened
- 1/2 avocado
- 1 scoop vanilla or chocolate isolate protein

- 1 cup spinach, fresh
- 1 cup ice

Optional:

- Cacao nibs

Directions :

1.   Put everything in a blender except the ice cubes. Blend for until smooth.
2.   Add in the ice cubes. Blend again.
3.   Pour in a glass. Enjoy!

****

Peppermint Patty

This smoothie taste like peppermint patty, but is packed with the nutritious goodness of spinach and almond milk. This drink is naturally sugar-free, Paleo-friendly, gluten-free, dairy-free, and vegan. This smoothie is thick and creamy with an ice cream-like goodness. Cocoa is rich in cholesterol lowering, cancer-fighting antioxidant polyphenols. Mint, on the other hand, is a natural energizer and digestive aid. You will love the minty, chocolatey sweetness of this smoothie.

Serves: 1
Prep. Time: 3 minutes
Blend Time: 2 minutes

Nutritional Facts

Serving Size: 319 g

Calories: 166
Total Fat: 5.1 g
Saturated Fat: 1.2 g   **Trans. Fat:** 0 g
Cholesterol: 0 mg
Sodium: 261 mg
Potassium: 529 mg
Total Carbohydrates: 9 g
Dietary Fiber: 5.3 g   **Sugar:** 0 g
Protein: 28 g

Vitamin A: 57%   **Vitamin C:** 14%

Calcium: 36%   **Iron:** 19%

Ingredients:

- 1/4 teaspoon mint extract
- 1 scoop chocolate isolate protein
- 1 cup unsweetened almond milk
- 1 cup spinach
- 2 tbsp. unsweetened cocoa powder
- Ice cubes

Directions:

1.   Put everything in a blender except the ice cubes. Blend for until smooth.
2.   Add in ice cubes. Blend again.
3.   Pour in a glass. Enjoy!

****

Blue-Raspberry Smoothie

Blueberries plus raspberries make this smoothie a powerhouse of antioxidants. Like blueberries, raspberries are rich in various antioxidants, such as vitamin C, gallic acid, and quercetin, which help fight circulatory and heart diseases, cancer, and other age-related conditions. Studies also show that eating whole berries are more beneficial than taking them in dietary supplement form.

Serves: 1

Prep. Time: 3 minutes

Blend Time: 2 minutes

Nutritional Facts

Serving Size: 470 g

Calories: 191

Total Fat: 5.6g

Saturated Fat: 0 g   **Trans. Fat:** 0 g

Cholesterol: 0 mg

Sodium: 325 mg

Potassium: 364 mg

Total Carbohydrates: 11.9 g

Dietary Fiber: 4.4 g   **Sugar:** 5 g

Protein: 26.1 g

Vitamin A: 0%   **Vitamin C:** 23%

Calcium: 47**%**   **Iron:** 12%

Ingredients:

- 1/4 cup blueberries, frozen
- 1/4 cup raspberries, frozen
- 1 1/2 cups unsweetened almond milk
- 1 pack gelatin or 1 scoop isolate protein

irections:

1.   Put all of the ingredients into the blender. Blend until smooth.

Kale, Spinach, and Strawberry Smoothie

Kale is a superfood that's packed with vitamins K, C, and A. The combination of Kale and Spinach make this smoothie a a super punch of nutrients!.

Serves: 2
Prep. Time: 3 minutes
Blend Time: 2 minutes

Nutritional Facts

Serving Size: 253 g

Calories: 156
Total Fat: 1.9 g
Saturated Fat: 0 g   **Trans. Fat:** 0 g
Cholesterol: 0 mg
Sodium: 186 mg
Potassium: 540 mg
Total Carbohydrates: 9.9 g
Dietary Fiber: 2.2 g   **Sugar:** 0.9 g
Protein: 27 g
Vitamin A: 234%   **Vitamin C:** 159%
Calcium: 27%   **Iron:** 12%

Ingredients:

- 2 cups kale
- 1 cup spinach
- 1/4 cup strawberries
- 1 cup unsweetened almond milk
- 2 packs gelatin

Directions:

1. Put all of the ingredients into the blender. Blend until smooth.

****

Green Power Smoothie

This smoothie is packed whole food goodness of kale, spinach, blueberries, strawberries, ginger, egg, and flax seeds. But what really makes this recipe is the rich texture of yogurt. Greek yogurt is packed with probiotics that helps keep a healthy balance of good bacteria in your digestive system. It's also packed with vitamin B12 that helps maintain healthy brain function.

Serves: 4

Prep. Time: 3 minutes

Blend Time: 2 minutes

Nutritional Facts

Serving Size: 255 g

Calories: 221

Total Fat: 4.1 g

Saturated Fat: 1.8 g   **Trans. Fat:** 0 g

Cholesterol: 45 mg

Sodium: 115 mg

Potassium: 345 mg

Total Carbohydrates: 11.3 g

Dietary Fiber: 2.4 g   **Sugar:** 6.5 g

Protein: 35.6 g

Vitamin A: 67%   **Vitamin C:** 66%

Calcium: 14%   **Iron:** 13%

Ingredients:

- 12 ounce Greek yogurt
- 1 cup spinach
- 1 cup kale
- 1/2 cup strawberry
- 1/2 cup blueberries

- 1 cup water
- 2 tbsp. flax seeds
- 1 tsp. ginger root, grated
- 1 egg
- 4 pack gelatin or 4 scoops isolate protein
- 1 ounce lemon zest

Directions :

1.   Put all of the ingredients into the blender. Blend until smooth.

****

Red Heart Smoothie

This red smoothie is packed flavonoids from the red cabbages, which also gives it's red color. The red cabbage is packed with vitamin C and 1 cup contains 56 percent of your body's daily recommended intake. Red cabbage also packs this smoothie with phytochemicals that help reduce the risk of heart disease, cancer, and other illnesses.

Serves: 2

Prep. Time: 3 minutes

Blend Time: 2 minutes

Nutritional Facts

Serving Size: 360 g

Calories: 1157

Total Fat: 0.7 g

Saturated Fat: 0 g   **Trans. Fat:** 0 g

Cholesterol: 0 mg

Sodium: 74 mg

Potassium: 2425 mg

Total Carbohydrates: 14.3 g

Dietary Fiber: 5.1 g   **Sugar:** 7.7 g

Protein: 26.3 g

Vitamin A: 20%   **Vitamin C:** 178%

Calcium: 5%   **Iron:** 16%

Ingredients:

- 5 medium strawberries
- 1/2 cup raspberries
- 1 cup red cabbage, chopped
- 1/2 red bell pepper
- 1 roma tomato
- 8 oz. cold water
- 1 ice cube **Directions:**

1.   Put all of the ingredients into the blender. Blend until smooth.

Orange-Carrot Smoothie

This smoothie is packed with the goodness of carrots, but tastes like oranges. Carrots pack this drink with beta-carotene or vitamin A. They are rich in fiber and are a good source of vitamins K, C, B8, folate, pantothenic acid, iron, potassium, manganese, and copper.

Serves: 3

Prep. Time: 3 minutes

Blend Time: 2 minutes

Nutritional Facts

Serving Size: 246 g

Calories: 137

Total Fat: 0.2 g

Saturated Fat: 0 g   **Trans. Fat:** 0 g

Cholesterol: 0 mg

Sodium: 84 mg

Potassium: 248 mg

Total Carbohydrates: 10.1 g

Dietary Fiber: 1.1 g   **Sugar:** 7 g

Protein: 24.7 g

Vitamin A: 123%   **Vitamin C:** 91%

Calcium: 3%   **Iron:** 7%

Ingredients:

- 1 cup sliced carrots
- 3/4 cup orange juice
- 1/2 teaspoon orange peel
- 3 pack gelatin or 3 scoops isolate protein
- 1 1/2 cups ice cubes

Directions:

1. Put all of the ingredients into the blender. Blend until smooth.

****

Super Green Smoothie

In this recipe we make an exception to oats and only add a little to add to the thickness of the smoothie. Oats are rich in soluble fiber that research shows they may help reduce the risk of coronary heart disease, colorectal cancer and blood pressure.

Serves: 5
Prep. Time: 3 minutes
Blend Time: 2 minutes

Nutritional Facts

Serving Size: 267 g

Calories: 141

Total Fat: 1.6 g

Saturated Fat: 0 g   **Trans. Fat:** 0 g

Cholesterol: 0 mg

Sodium: 77 mg

Potassium: 376 mg

Total Carbohydrates: 12.9 g

Dietary Fiber: 2.9 g   **Sugar:** 4.8 g

Protein: 21.6 g

Vitamin A: 10%   **Vitamin C:** 18%

Calcium: 9%   **Iron:** 10%

Ingredients:

- 6 ounces unsweetened almond milk
- 3 tablespoon rolled oats
- 1 cup spinach
- 2 strawberries
- 1/2 cup blueberries
- 1/2 stalk celery
- 3 slices cucumber
- 1 teaspoon cinnamon
- 1 tablespoon flax seed
- 1 tablespoon cocoa powder
- 4 pack gelatin

Directions:

1.   Put all of the ingredients into the blender. Blend until smooth.

****

Superfood Smoothie

Spinach is a well-known super food by now that is packed with amazing health benefits which includes improving the blood glucose control and bone health, lowering the rick of asthma and blood pressure. Spinach also contains alpha-lipoic acid or ALA which helps to lower glucose level and increase insulin sensitivity.

Serves: 2
Prep. Time: 3 minutes
Blend Time: 2 minutes

Nutritional Facts

Serving Size: 304 g

Calories: 318

Total Fat: 14.6 g

Saturated Fat: 3.3 g   **Trans. Fat:** 0 g

Cholesterol: 3 mg

Sodium: 156 mg

Potassium: 595 mg

Total Carbohydrates: 16.7 g

Dietary Fiber: 7.3 g   **Sugar:** 7.2 g

Protein: 32.5 g

Vitamin A: 30%   **Vitamin C:** 49%

Calcium: 21%   **Iron:** 22%

Ingredients:

- 100 g Greek yogurt
- 1/2 avocado
- 1/3 cup strawberries, frozen
- 1/2 cup blueberries, frozen
- 3/4 cup unsweetened almond milk
- 2 tablespoons flax seed
- 1 cup spinach
- 2 packs gelatin

Directions :

1.   Put all of the ingredients into the blender. Blend until smooth.

****

Silken Tofu Smoothie

Strawberries, tofu, and almond combine to make a simple yet very satisfying creamy smoothie that is naturally high in protein. Makes for an greatt post workout smoothie!

Serves: 2
Prep. Time: 3 minutes
Blend Time: 2 minutes

Nutritional Facts

Serving Size: 225 g

Calories: 145
Total Fat: 3.0 g
Saturated Fat: 0 g   **Trans. Fat:** 0 g
Cholesterol: 0 mg
Sodium: 133 mg
Potassium: 234 mg
Total Carbohydrates: 12.9 g
Dietary Fiber: 1.3 g   **Sugar:** 10.3 g
Protein: 15.6 g
Vitamin A: 0%   **Vitamin C:** 35%
Calcium: 18%   **Iron:** 6%

Ingredients:

- 1/2 cup strawberries, unfrozen
- 1 slice silken tofu
- 1 cup unsweetened almond milk, vanilla
- Pinch of cinnamon
- 1 packet stevia or 2 teaspoons Splenda

Directions :

2.   Put everything in a blender. Blend for until smooth. Pour in a glass. Enjoy!

****

Carrot and Leafy Green Smoothie

Super greens, carrots, and peaches make this a refreshing smoothie that is packed with vitamin A and antioxidants . Perfect on a hot summer day!

Serves: 2
Net Carb: 10.4 g
Prep. Time: 3 minutes
Blend Time: 2 minutes

Nutritional Facts

Serving Size: 274g

Calories: 173
Total Fat: 2.2 g
Saturated Fat: 0 g   **Trans. Fat:** 0 g
Cholesterol: 0 mg
Sodium: 133 mg
Potassium: 375 mg
Total Carbohydrates: 13.8 g
Dietary Fiber: 3.4 g   **Sugar:** 9.4 g
Protein: 26.1 g
Vitamin A: 120%   **Vitamin C:** 23%
Calcium: 12%   **Iron:** 11%

Ingredients:

- 1/2 cup peach slices, frozen
- 1 medium carrot
- 1/2 cup green grapes
- 1/2 cup spinach
- 1/2 cup green cabbage
- 1/2 cup unsweetened almond milk
- 1 tablespoon ground flaxseeds
- 1/2 cup ice cubes
- 2 pack gelatin

Directions :

1. Put all of the ingredients into the blender. Blend until smooth.

****

This smoothie takes a bit of effort, but it will definitely be worth it. Green tea pairs with other flavors well. The combination of carrots, mango, and ginger makes for an exotic tasting smoothie.

Serves: 4

Prep. Time: 35 minutes

Blend Time: 2 minutes

Nutritional Facts

Serving Size: 276 g

Calories: 149

Total Fat: 0.8 g

Saturated Fat: 0 g   **Trans. Fat:** 0 g

Cholesterol: 0 mg

Sodium: 81 mg

Potassium: 198 mg

Total Carbohydrates: 11.6 g

Dietary Fiber: 2 g   **Sugar:** 8.2 g

Protein: 24.8 g

Vitamin A: 970%   **Vitamin C:** 19%

Calcium: 4%   **Iron:** 6%

Ingredients:

- 5 ounces mango, frozen
- 1 cup carrots
- 1-inch tablespoon ginger, pounded
- 4 green tea bags
- 1 teaspoon honey
- 1 tablespoon chia seeds or flax seeds

- 4 pack gelatin
- 3 cups water

Directions :

1.   In a small saucepan, pour water. Bring water to a boil. Add in the carrots. Cover. Cook for about 10-15 minutes or until the carrots are tender. Add in the ginger during the last 2 minutes of cooking.

2.   Remove the saucepan from the heat. Add in the tea bags. Cover. Steep for 4 minutes. Remove the tea bags, squeezing out all the tea. Remove the ginger. Place the pan on a hot pad in the refrigerator for 10 minutes.

3.   Transfer the carrot mixture into a blender. Add in the mango. Add in the chia or flax seeds.

4.   Blend until smooth. Serve.

Devilishly Delicious Smoothies

These smoothies are keto-friendly desserts in a cup! You can have these delicious drinks without worrying about having too many carbs. Just keep in mind what your target marco's are for the day and enjoy!

Creamy Chocolate Milkshake

This is a quick and easy way to make your own keto friendly chocolate milkshake. This low carb version is delicious but because you can eat a lot of fat you can enjoy it guilt free!

Serves: 2
Prep. Time: 3 minutes
Blend Time: 2 minutes

Nutritional Facts

Serving Size: 361 g

Calories: 120
Total Fat: 24.2 g
Saturated Fat: 13.3 g   **Trans. Fat:** 0 g
Cholesterol: 78 mg
Sodium: 214 mg
Potassium: 218 mg
Total Carbohydrates: 7.4 g
Dietary Fiber: 0.9 g   **Sugar:** 4.1 g
Protein: 14.1 g
Vitamin A: 17%   **Vitamin C:** 1%
Calcium: 32%   **Iron:** 5%

Ingredients:

- 16 ounces unsweetened almond milk, vanilla
- 4 ounces heavy cream
- 1 scoop chocolate isolate protein
- 1 packet stevia or 2 teaspoons Splenda
- 1/2 cup crushed ice

Directions :

1. Put everything in a blender except the ice cubes. Blend for until smooth.
2. Add in the ice cubes. Blend again.
3. Pour in a glass. Enjoy!

***

Espresso Smoothie

You'll love the aroma and bold, bitter flavor of this drink. Coffee not only keeps you awake, but there is research that shows drinking a cup of Joe increases insulin sensitivity due to its mineral content of chromium and magnesium., These are known to stimulate insulin uptake in the cells. Coffee is also a great source of antioxidants, which are known to lower risks of inflammatory conditions, such as Alzheimer's and Parkinson's disease.

Serves: 1

Prep. Time: 3 minutes

Blend Time: 2 minutes

<u>**Nutritional Facts**</u>

Serving Size: 338 g

Calories: 186

Total Fat: 1.4 g

Saturated Fat: 1.0 g   Trans. Fat: 0 g

Cholesterol: 3 mg

Sodium: 81 mg

Potassium: 214 mg

Total Carbohydrates: 10.9 g

Dietary Fiber: 0 g   Sugar: 10.6 g

Protein: 30.8 g

Vitamin A: 0%   Vitamin C: 0%

Calcium: 9%   Iron: 2%

Ingredients:

- 1/4 cup (65 g) Greek yogurt, full-fat
- 1 espresso shot or 1 cup black coffee
- 1 scoop vanilla isolate protein or 2 tablespoons gelatin plus 1 teaspoon vanilla extract
- 1/2 packet stevia or 1 teaspoons Splenda
- Pinch of cinnamon
- 5 ice cubes

Directions :

- Put everything in a blender except the ice cubes. Blend for until smooth.
- Add in the ice cubes. Blend again.

- Pour in a glass. Enjoy!

****

Hazelnut Keto Coffee Smoothie

This smoothie combines hazelnut flavor and coffee into a delicious dessert that will start your day off with a tasty bang!

Serves: 1

Prep. Time: 3 minutes

Blend Time: 2 minutes

Nutritional Facts

Serving Size: 286 g

Calories: 19

Total Fat: 20.6 g

Saturated Fat: 9.6 g   **Trans. Fat:** 0 g

Cholesterol: 55 mg

Sodium: 20 mg

Potassium: 210 mg

Total Carbohydrates: 2.7 g

Dietary Fiber: 0.9 g   **Sugar:** 0 g

Protein: 2.5 g

Vitamin A: 12%   **Vitamin C:** 1%

Calcium: 4%   **Iron:** 3%

Ingredients:

- 1/3 cup heavy cream
- 1 cup cold coffee
- 1-2 tablespoon hazelnut syrup, sugar-free
- Ice cubes

Directions :

1.   Put everything in a blender except the ice cubes. Blend for until smooth.
2.   Add in ice cubes. Blend again.
3.   Pour in a glass. Enjoy!

****

The Peanut Milkshake

Peanut butter is not just for your kid's lunch! This versatile spread is high in healthy oils and protein, which help aid weight loss, diabetes, and Alzheimer's disease. Peanuts also contain fiber for a healthy bowel movement, magnesium for muscle and bone health.

Serves: 2
Prep. Time: 3 minutes
Blend Time: 2 minutes

Nutritional Facts

Serving Size: 326g

Calories: 278
Total Fat: 24.1 g
Saturated Fat: 14.5 g   **Trans. Fat:** 0 g
Cholesterol: 0 mg
Sodium: 176 mg
Potassium: 361 mg
Total Carbohydrates: 11.7g
Dietary Fiber: 2.8 g   **Sugar:** 7.8 g
Protein: 5.9 g
Vitamin A: 0%   **Vitamin C:** 3%
Calcium: 16%   **Iron:** 16%

Ingredients:

- 2 tablespoons peanut butter, all-natural
- 1 tsp vanilla extract
- 1 packet stevia or 2 teaspoons Splenda
- 1 cup unsweetened almond milk, vanilla
- 1/2 cup coconut milk, regular
- 1 cup ice cubes

Directions :

1.   Put everything in a blender except the ice cubes. Blend for until smooth.
2.   Add in ice cubes. Blend again.
3.   Pour in a glass. Enjoy!

****

The Keto Frapp

This dairy-free, sugar-free, completely keto and vegan-friendly smoothie is a great way to kick off your fat-burning morning. This simple and tasty drink sneaks added nutrients in with grounded flax seeds.

Serves: 1

Prep. Time: 3 minutes

Blend Time: 2 minutes

Nutritional Facts

Serving Size: 295 g

Calories: 226

Total Fat: 19.5 g

Saturated Fat: 9.8 g   **Trans. Fat:** 0 g

Cholesterol: 55 mg

Sodium: 24 mg

Potassium: 266 mg

Total Carbohydrates: 5.7 g   **Dietary:** 0g

Fiber: 3.8 g   **Sugar:** 0.8 g

Protein: 3.7 g

Vitamin A: 12%   **Vitamin C:** 0%

Calcium: 4%   **Iron:** 22%

Ingredients:

- 1 cup leftover or cold coffee
- 1 teaspoon vanilla extract
- 1/3 cup heavy cream
- 1-2 tablespoons ground flax seeds
- 6 ice cubes

Optional: for a sweeter blend

      • 2 tablespoons salted caramel syrup, sugar-free

Directions :

1.   Put everything in a blender except the ice cubes. Blend for until smooth.
2.   Add in ice cubes. Blend again.
3.   Pour in a glass.
4.   Add caramel syrup, if desired. Enjoy!

****

Apricot, Peach, and Coconut Smoothie

Apricots blend well with coconut and other tropical fruits. Blending them with peaches and coconut milk is a yummy alternative.

Serves: 4
Prep. Time: 3 minutes
Blend Time: 2 minutes

Nutritional Facts

Serving Size: 230g

Calories: 236
Total Fat: 10.6 g
Saturated Fat: 9 g   **Trans. Fat:** 0 g
Cholesterol: 0 mg
Sodium: 64 mg
Potassium: 348 mg
Total Carbohydrates: 12.8 g
Dietary Fiber: 2.7 g   **Sugar:** 10.2 g
Protein: 26.1 g
Vitamin A: 25%   **Vitamin C:** 16%
Calcium: 3%   **Iron:** 7%

Ingredients:

- 6 ounces coconut milk
- 1 cup peaches
- 1 1/2 cup apricot
- 4 pack gelatin
- 1 cup ice cubes

Directions :

1.   Put all of the ingredients into the blender. Blend until smooth.

****

Rich n' Creamy Blackberry Smoothie

Blackberries make this smoothie rich in Vitamin C and bioflavonoids. These berries have one of the highest antioxidant levels of all fruits, which give them their dark blue color. Bioflavonoids help make the skin look younger, keeps the brain alert, and helps maintain your memory. Blueberries are also high in tannin, which helps you 'down there' by helping to alleviate hemorrhoids, reduce inflammation in the intestine, and soothe diarrhea.

Serves: 2

Prep. Time: 3 minutes

Blend Time: 2 minutes

Nutritional Facts

Serving Size: 268 g

Calories: 300

Total Fat17 g

Saturated Fat: 10.4 g   Trans. Fat: 0 g

Cholesterol: 62 mg

Sodium: 76 mg

Potassium: 156 mg

Total Carbohydrates: 12.2 g

Dietary Fiber: 3.8 g   Sugar: 7.6 g

Protein: 25.9 g

Vitamin A: 16%   Vitamin C: 26%

Calcium: 7%   Iron: 4%

Ingredients:

- 1 cup fresh blackberries
- 1 packet stevia or 2 teaspoons Splenda
- 3/4 cup heavy whipping cream
- 2 scoops vanilla isolate protein or 4 tablespoons gelatin plus
2 teaspoon vanilla extract
- 1 cup ice cubes

Directions :

1.   Put everything in a blender except the ice cubes.
    Blend for until smooth.
2.   Add in ice cubes. Blend again.
3.   Pour in a glass. Enjoy!

****

Cinnamon Roll Smoothie

This delicious smoothie contains Chia seeds, which are packed with nutrients. In fact, chia is an ancient Mayan word for "strength". These seeds are loaded with protein, fiber, omega 3 fatty acids, and other micronutrients. They are also rich in calcium, magnesium, manganese, and phosphorus.

Serves: 1
Prep. Time: 3 minutes
Blend Time: 2 minutes

Nutritional Facts

Serving Size: 532 g

Calories: 217
Total Fat: 24.2 g
Saturated Fat: 0.6 g   **Trans. Fat:** 0 g
Cholesterol: 0 mg
Sodium: 244 mg
Potassium: 260 mg
Total Carbohydrates: 13.1 g
Dietary Fiber: 3.5 g   **Sugar:** 8.2 g
Protein: 26.3 g
Vitamin A: 0%   **Vitamin C:** 0%
Calcium: 34%   **Iron:** 17%

Ingredients:

- 1/4 tsp vanilla extract
- 1/2 tsp cinnamon
- 1 cup unsweetened almond milk
- 1 packet stevia
- 1 tbsp. chia seeds or flax seeds
- 2 tbsp. vanilla protein powder or 2 tablespoons gelatin plus 1 teaspoon vanilla extract
- 1 cup ice cubes

Directions :

1.   Put everything in a blender except the ice cubes. Blend for until smooth.
2.   Add in the ice cubes. Blend again.
3.   Pour in a glass. Enjoy!

****

Yummy Strawberry-Cheesecake Smoothie

This simple creamy thick smoothie is sweet and has an indulgent strawberry cheesecake flavor that will satisfy your taste buds. The secret of this drink is the goodness of cream cheese, which gives it that creamy tang taste that we all love.

Serves: 2

Prep. Time: 3 minutes

Blend Time: 2 minutes

Nutritional Facts

Serving Size: 138 g

Calories: 164
Total Fat: 10.8 g
Saturated Fat: 6.3 g   **Trans. Fat:** 0 g
Cholesterol: 31 mg
Sodium: 129 mg
Potassium: 83 mg
Total Carbohydrates: 12.6 g
Dietary Fiber: 1 g   **Sugar:** 10.4 g
Protein: 2.4 g
Vitamin A: 8%   **Vitamin C:** 23%
Calcium: 10%   **Iron:** 4%

Ingredients:

- 1/2 cup frozen strawberries, unsweetened
- 1/2 cup unsweetened almond milk, vanilla
- 1/2 teaspoons vanilla extract
- 2 ounces cream cheese, regular
- 2 packets stevia or 4 teaspoons Splenda
- 3-4 ice cubes

Directions :

1.   Put everything in a blender except the ice cubes.
   Blend for until smooth.
2.   Add in ice cubes. Blend again.

3.   Pour in a glass. Enjoy!

Mango Berry Slush

This blend is a deliciously tart and sweet drink that is packed with vitamin C. This berry flavored slushy is a refreshing low-carb, high protein drink that everyone will love.

Serves: 4
Prep. Time: 3 minutes
Blend Time: 2 minutes

Nutritional Facts

Serving Size: 281 g

Calories: 128
Total Fat: 0.2 g
Saturated Fat: 0 g   **Trans. Fat:** 0 g
Cholesterol: 0 mg
Sodium: 60 mg
Potassium: 117 mg
Total Carbohydrates: 8.5 g
Dietary Fiber: 1.3 g   **Sugar:** 6.2 g
Protein: 24.4 g
Vitamin A: 5%   **Vitamin C:** 54%
Calcium: 4%   **Iron:** 3%

Ingredients:

- 4 ounces' mango
- 1 cup strawberries
- 1 1/2 cups carbonated water
- 1 1/2 cups ice
- 4 pack gelatin
- 1 lime

Directions :

1.   Put all of the ingredients into the blender. Blend until smooth.

*****

Raspberry Cheesecake Blend

Like the Strawberry-Cheesecake Smoothie, this version is a yummy smoothie with a creamy, sweet cheesecake flavor. The cottage cheese adds protein to the blend and keeps the carbs low. The protein content of this cheese is casein, which make you feel full longer and helps build muscle.

Serves: 1

Prep. Time: 3 minutes

Blend Time: 2 minutes

<u>Nutritional Facts</u>

Serving Size: 353 g

Calories: 208

Total Fat: 13.8 g

Saturated Fat: 6.5 g   **Trans. Fat:** 0 g

Cholesterol: 31 mg

Sodium: 266 mg

Potassium: 336 mg

Total Carbohydrates: 11.7 g

Dietary Fiber: 5.0 g   **Sugar:** 4.4 g

Protein: 3.9 g

Vitamin A: 8%   **Vitamin C:** 27%

Calcium: 34%   **Iron:** 8%

Ingredients:

- 1 cup unsweetened almond milk
- 1/2 cup raspberries
- 1 ounce cream cheese
- 1 tablespoon vanilla syrup, sugar-free
- 4 Ice cubes

Directions :

1.   Put everything in a blender except the ice cubes.
      Blend for until smooth.
2.   Add in ice cubes. Blend again.

3.   Pour in a glass. Enjoy!

Strawberry-Almond Crunch Smoothie

Adding almond nuts to a strawberry smoothie gives it a delicious crunchy texture. It also packs the smoothie the nutrients L-carnitine (known for its weight loss properties) and riboflavin, which help boost brain activity and reduce the risk of Alzheimer's disease.

Serves: 1

Prep. Time: 3 minutes

Blend Time: 2 minutes

<u>Nutritional Facts</u>

Serving Size: 335 g

Calories: 135

Total Fat: 9.7 g

Saturated Fat: 0.8 g   Trans. Fat: 0 g

Cholesterol: 0 mg

Sodium: 181 mg

Potassium: 392 mg

Total Carbohydrates: 11 g

Dietary Fiber: 4.5 g   Sugar: 4 g

Protein: 4 g

Vitamin A: 0%   Vitamin C: 71%

Calcium: 36%   Iron: 9%

Ingredients:

- 2 tablespoons almonds
- 1/2 teaspoon cinnamon
- 1/2 cup organic strawberries, frozen
- 1 cup unsweetened almond milk, vanilla
- 2 iced cubes

Optional:

- 1 tablespoon chia seeds or flax seeds

Directions:

1.   Put everything in a blender. Blend for until smooth. Pour in a glass., add iced cubes and enjoy!

****

Peach Pie Shake

This aromatic smoothie is sweet and tangy. Peach is a good source of vitamin A that helps improve vision and helps fight free radicals. Vitamins A and C keeps skin healthy – moisturized, glowing, supple, and soft. Regularly eating peaches also help increase the blood circulation of the body.

Serves: 1
Prep. Time: 3 minutes
Blend Time: 2 minutes

Nutritional Facts

Serving Size: 358 g

Calories: 209
Total Fat: 3.9 g
Saturated Fat: 1.2 g   **Trans. Fat:** 0 g
Cholesterol: 3 mg
Sodium: 196 mg
Potassium: 412 mg
Total Carbohydrates: 13.8 g
Dietary Fiber: 2.5 g   **Sugar:** 10.8 g
Protein: 32.1 g
Vitamin A: 7%   **Vitamin C:** 11%
Calcium: 29%   **Iron:** 6%

Ingredients:

- 1 peach, pitted
- 1 scoop vanilla protein powder or 2 tablespoons gelatin plus 1 teaspoon vanilla extract
- 1/4 cup plain Greek yogurt
- 2 pinches of cinnamon
- 2/3 cup unsweetened almond milk
- 8-10 ice cubes

Directions:

- Put everything in a blender except the ice cubes. Blend for until smooth.
- Add in the ice cubes. Blend again.
- Pour in a glass. Enjoy!

****

Buttered Pumpkin Pie Coffee

While most of the pumpkin-flavored treats should be enjoyed occasionally, you can sip on this low carb smoothie everyday. Plus this guilt-free smoothie is packed with 102% of your daily intake of vitamin A.

Serves: 1
Prep. Time: 3 minutes
Blend Time: 2 minutes

Nutritional Facts

Serving Size: 393 g

Calories: 157
Total Fat: 11.7 g
Saturated Fat: 7.4 g   **Trans. Fat:** 0 g
Cholesterol: 31 mg
Sodium: 90 mg
Potassium: 236 mg
Total Carbohydrates: 10.8 g
Dietary Fiber: 0.9 g   **Sugar:** 9.1 g
Protein: 0.9 g
Vitamin A: 102%   **Vitamin C:** 2%
Calcium: 2%   **Iron:** 3%

Ingredients:

- 1/4 teaspoon pumpkin pie spice
- 1 tablespoon regular butter, unsalted
- 12 ounces hot coffee
- 2 tablespoons canned pumpkin
- 1 packet stevia or 2 teaspoons Splenda

Directions:

- Put everything in a blender. Blend for until smooth. Pour in a glass. Enjoy!

****

Chocolate-Cayenne Shake

This smoothie is a unique treat. This cold blend is spiked with the surprising touch of cayenne heat. Cayenne is a spice known to neutralize acidity and stimulate circulation. This makes it a well-known ingredient in detoxifying and cleansing regimes.

Serves: 2

Prep. Time: 3 minutes

Blend Time: 2 minutes

<u>Nutritional Facts</u>

Serving Size: 171 g

Calories: 218

Total Fat: 22.6 g

Saturated Fat: 18.7 g   Trans. Fat: 0 g

Cholesterol: 0 mg

Sodium: 10 mg

Potassium: 246 mg

Total Carbohydrates: 5.8 g

Dietary Fiber: 3.3 g   Sugar: 1.2 g

Protein: 2.3 g

Vitamin A: 1%   Vitamin C: 2%

Calcium: 2%   Iron: 13%

Ingredients:

- 1/4 cup coconut cream
- 1/2 - 1 cup water
- 1/2 pinch cayenne powder
- 1 tbsp. flax seeds or chia seeds
- 2 tbsp. unsweetened cocoa powder
- 2 tbsp. unrefined coconut oil
- Dash of vanilla extract
- Pinch of ground cinnamon
- Ice cubes, if desired

Directions:

1.   Put everything in a blender except the ice cubes. Blend for until smooth.
2.   Add in the ice cubes. Blend again.
3.   Pour in a glass. Enjoy!

Peanut Butter Crunch Chocolate Smoothie

This creamy thick smoothie is a nutritious breakfast or as an indulgent snack. This smoothie will fuel you and satisfy your sweet tooth.

Serves: 2
Prep. Time: 3 minutes
Blend Time: 2 minutes

Nutritional Facts

Serving Size: 338 g

Calories: 186
Total Fat: 1.4 g
Saturated Fat: 1 g   **Trans. Fat:** 0 g
Cholesterol: 3 mg
Sodium: 81 mg
Potassium: 214 mg
Total Carbohydrates: 10.9 g
Dietary Fiber: 0 g   **Sugar:** 10.6 g
Protein: 30.8 g
Vitamin A: 0%   **Vitamin C:** 0%
Calcium: 9%   **Iron:** 2%

Ingredients:

- 1 1/2 cups unsweetened almond milk
- 1 scoop chocolate whey protein powder 2 tablespoons gelatin plus 1 tablespoon unsweetened cocoa powder
- 1 packet stevia or 2 teaspoons Splenda
- 2 tablespoons peanut butter, organic
- 1/2 cup ice

Directions :

1.   Put everything in a blender. Blend for until smooth. Adjust sweetness according to taste.
2.   Pour in a glass. Enjoy!

****

Whipped Chocolate Shake

Whipping cream makes this shake light as air and creamy. This out of this world sensational drink is also high is calcium.

Serves: 1

Prep. Time: 3 minutes

Blend Time: 2 minutes

Nutritional Facts

Serving Size: 306 g

Calories: 236
Total Fat: 19 g
Saturated Fat: 10 g   **Trans. Fat:** 0 g
Cholesterol: 55 mg
Sodium: 197 mg
Potassium: 305 mg
Total Carbohydrates: 14.3 g
Dietary Fiber: 2.8 g   **Sugar:** 8.4g
Protein: 2.9 g
Vitamin A: 12%   **Vitamin C:** 0%
Calcium: 33%   **Iron:** 8%

Ingredients:

- 1 cup unsweetened almond milk
- 1/3 cup heavy whipping cream
- 1 packet stevia or 2 teaspoons Splenda
- 1/2 teaspoon vanilla extract
- 1 tablespoon unsweetened cocoa powder
- 3 ice cubes

Directions :

1.   Put everything in a blender except the ice cubes. Blend for until smooth.

2.   Add in ice cubes. Blend again.

3.   Pour in a glass. Enjoy!

Mango Almond Smoothie

Here's a simple, easy, healthy, yet delicious vegan and low fat smoothie. Research shows that mangoes are packed with antioxidants that help protect against leukemia, breast, colon, and prostate cancer. Mangoes are also high in pectin, fiber, and vitamin C that lower LDL or bad cholesterol. They also help keep the skin clear, improve eye health, improve digestion, and boost the immune system.

Serves: 2
Prep. Time: 3 minutes
Blend Time: 2 minutes

Nutritional Facts
Serving Size: 233 g

Calories: 124
Total Fat: 2.6 g
Saturated Fat: 0 g   **Trans. Fat:** 0 g
Cholesterol: 0 mg
Sodium: 99 mg
Potassium: 200 mg
Total Carbohydrates: 12.4 g
Dietary Fiber: 2.5 g   **Sugar:** 9.4 g
Protein: 25.3 g
Vitamin A: 10%   **Vitamin C:** 29%

Calcium: 14%   **Iron:** 9%

Ingredients:

- 125 g mango, frozen
- 3/4 cup unsweetened almond milk
- 1 pack gelatin or 1 scoop isolate protein
- 1 tablespoon flax seeds
- 1/2 cup ice cubes

Directions :

1.   Put all of the ingredients into the blender. Blend until smooth.

****

Almond Strawberry Smoothie

This crunchy version is packed with protein and blends the delicious flavors and has heart-healthy nutrients which makes it a great dairy-free smoothie. This drink is refreshingly nutty and smooth.

Serves: 2

Prep. Time: 3 minutes

Blend Time: 2 minutes

Nutritional Facts

Serving Size: 272 g

Calories: 162

Total Fat: 5.7 g

Saturated Fat: 0 g   **Trans. Fat:** 0 g

Cholesterol: 0 mg

Sodium: 218 mg

Potassium: 230 mg

Total Carbohydrates: 3.8 g

Dietary Fiber: 1.8 g   **Sugar:** 0.8 g

Protein: 26 g

Vitamin A: 0%   **Vitamin C:** 12%

Calcium: 30%   **Iron:** 7%

Ingredients:

- 16 ounces unsweetened Almond milk
- 8 almonds
- 2 large strawberry, frozen
- 1 1/2 scoop whey protein powder or 3 tablespoon gelatin
- 6 ice cubes

Directions :

1.   Put all of the ingredients into the blender. Blend until smooth.

****

Chocolate Avocado Cream Smoothie

The avocado in this smoothie makes for a sinfully delicious drink. Rich, creamy, and velvety smooth. The avocado also packs this drink with a healthy amount of good fats.

Serves: 2
Prep. Time: 3 minutes
Blend Time: 2 minutes

Nutritional Facts

Serving Size: 286 g

Calories: 450
Total Fat: 32.3 g
Saturated Fat: 12.1 g   **Trans. Fat:** 0 g
Cholesterol: 42 mg
Sodium: 53 mg
Potassium: 535 mg
Total Carbohydrates: 16.6 g
Dietary Fiber: 6.9 g **Sugar:** 7.2 g
Protein: 26.9 g
Vitamin A: 12%   **Vitamin C:** 17%
Calcium: 6%   **Iron:** 6%

Ingredients:

- 1 avocado, frozen
- 1/2 cup heavy cream
- 1 tablespoons dark chocolate
- 1 teaspoon Splenda
- 1 pack gelatin or 1 scoop chocolate isolate protein
- 1 cup water

Directions :

1.   Put all of the ingredients into the blender. Blend until smooth

****

Very Berry Strawberry Smoothie

The secret to a thick frosty smoothie is using frozen fruits and nearly frozen milk. This drink is loaded with flavors and vitamins and is best served on a warm summer day.

Serves: 1

Prep. Time: 3 minutes

Blend Time: 2 minutes

Nutritional Facts

Serving Size: 249 g

Calories: 197

Total Fat: 3 g	**Saturated Fat:** 1 g	**Trans. Fat:** 0 g

Cholesterol: 3 mg

Sodium: 163 mg

Potassium: 224 mg

Total Carbohydrates: 11.5 g

Dietary Fiber: 1.8 g	**Sugar:** 8.8 g

Protein: 30.4 g

Vitamin A: 0%	**Vitamin C:** 13%
Calcium: 23%	**Iron:** 5%

Ingredients:

- 2 ounces Greek yogurt, strawberry
- 1/4 cup berries, frozen
- 1/2 cup unsweetened almond milk
- 1 teaspoon Splenda
- 1 pack gelatin or 1 scoop isolate protein

Directions :

1.   Put all of the ingredients into the blender. Blend until smooth.

****

Peach Coconut Smoothie

Fresh summer peaches and coconut milk make this a sweet, creamy dairy-free blend. Using chilled coconut milk gives it a milkshake-like consistency. The coconut milk also makes it extra rich and creamy with the high amount of healthy fats.

Serves: 2
Prep. Time: 3 minutes
Blend Time: 2 minutes

Nutritional Facts

Serving Size: 342 g

Calories: 399
Total Fat: 28.8 g
Saturated Fat: 25.4 g   **Trans. Fat:** 0 g
Cholesterol: 0 mg
Sodium: 76 mg
Potassium: 464 mg
Total Carbohydrates: 13.9 g
Dietary Fiber: 3.8 g   **Sugar:** 10.2 g
Protein: 27.4 g
Vitamin A: 5%   **Vitamin C:** 16%
Calcium: 4%   **Iron:** 14%
Ingredients:

- 1 1/2 peaches, frozen
- 1 cup coconut milk
- 1 tsp. lemon zest
- 2 pack gelatin
- 1 cup ice

Directions :

1.   Put all of the ingredients into the blender. Blend until smooth.

****

Coconut-Strawberry Smoothie

With just 5 ingredients, this dairy-free smoothie is creamy and sweet. The vanilla makes this blend taste like ice cream. I love to add a little bit of unsweetened shredded coconut after blending for added flavor.

Serves: 1

Prep. Time: 3 minutes

Blend Time: 2 minutes

Nutritional Facts

Serving Size: 219 g

Calories: 438

Total Fat: 31 g

Saturated Fat: 25.7 g   **Trans. Fat:** 0 g

Cholesterol: 0 mg

Sodium: 76 mg

Potassium: 475 mg

Total Carbohydrates: 13.8 g

Dietary Fiber: 5.7 g   **Sugar:** 7.6 g

Protein: 28.4 g

Vitamin A: 0%   **Vitamin C:** 64%

Calcium: 5%   **Iron:** 25%

Ingredients:

- 5 strawberries, frozen
- 1 cup unsweetened coconut milk
- 1 tablespoon ground flax seed
- 1 pack gelatin or 1 scoop isolate protein
- 1 teaspoon vanilla extract

Directions :

1.   Put all of the ingredients into the blender. Blend until smooth.

****

Cocoa-Coconut-Macadamia Smoothie

If you haven't tried creamy, crunchy macadamia nuts, then it's about time you do! These nuts are high in heart-healthy omega 3 fatty acids, which are also important for the nervous system and fights inflammation.

Serves: 2
Prep. Time: 3 minutes
Blend Time: 2 minutes

Nutritional Facts

Serving Size: 236 g

Calories: 240
Total Fat: 12.4 g
Saturated Fat: 2.1 g   **Trans. Fat:** 0 g
Cholesterol: 0 mg
Sodium: 321 mg
Potassium: 172 mg
Total Carbohydrates: 8.3 g
Dietary Fiber: 2.5 g   **Sugar:** 4.8 g
Protein: 26 g
Vitamin A: 0%   **Vitamin C:** 0%
Calcium: 15%   **Iron:** 8%

Ingredients:

- 1 ounce (2 tbsp.) ground macadamia nuts
- 3/4 cup unsweetened almond milk
- 1 tablespoon unsweetened cocoa powder
- 2 teaspoons Splenda
- 1/2 teaspoon vanilla extract
- 1 g salt
- 2 pack gelatin
- 1 cup ice cubes

Directions :

1. Put all of the ingredients into the blender. Blend until smooth.

****

Chocolate-Coconut Tofu Smoothie

This high fat, high protein smoothie tastes like a chocolate milkshake. The tofu makes this smoothie silky smooth, almost like pudding. This drink is a yummy way to start the day!

Serves: 1

Prep. Time: 3 minutes

Blend Time: 2 minutes

Nutritional Facts

Serving Size: 395 g

Calories: 401

Total Fat: 25.4 g

Saturated Fat: 18.7 g   **Trans. Fat:** 0 g

Cholesterol: 0 mg

Sodium: 88 mg

Potassium: 488 mg

Total Carbohydrates: 13.6 g

Dietary Fiber: 4.7 g   **Sugar:** 7.6 g

Protein: 37.2 g

Vitamin A: 0%   **Vitamin C:** 4%

Calcium: 29%   **Iron:** 25%

Ingredients:

- 80 ml unsweetened coconut milk
- 1/2 cup tofu, silken
- 1 tablespoon unsweetened cocoa powder
- 150 ml water
- 1 teaspoon Splenda
- 1 pack gelatin or 1 scoop isolate protein

Directions :

1.   Put all of the ingredients into the blender. Blend until smooth.

****

Almond Chocolate Blueberry Smoothie

This blend is as almost as rich tasting and creamy as a classic milkshake, only this version is low carb! The blueberries and cocoa powder boost the antioxidant properties of this smoothie.

Serves: 1
Prep. Time: 3 minutes
Blend Time: 2 minutes

Nutritional Facts

Serving Size: 324 g

Calories: 185
Total Fat: 4.4 g
Saturated Fat: 0.8 g   **Trans. Fat:** 0 g
Cholesterol: 0 mg
Sodium: 236 mg
Potassium: 306 mg
Total Carbohydrates: 13.3 g
Dietary Fiber: 3.7 g   **Sugar:** 6.8 g
Protein: 26.3 g
Vitamin A: 0%   **Vitamin C:** 10%
Calcium: 32%   **Iron:** 13%

Ingredients:

- 1 cup unsweetened almond milk
- 1/4 cup blueberries, frozen
- 1/4 tsp vanilla extract
- 1 tablespoon unsweetened cocoa powder
- 1 teaspoon Splenda
- 1 pack gelatin or 1 scoop isolate protein

Directions :

1.   Put all of the ingredients into the blender. Blend until smooth.

****

Just Peachy Smoothies

This blend is a refreshing, healthy smoothie that is packed with protein. When in season, I love to substitute the blueberries with peach for a change in color and flavor.

Serves: 4

Prep. Time: 3 minutes

Blend Time: 2 minutes

Nutritional Facts

Serving Size: 255 g

Calories: 181

Total Fat: 2.3 g

Saturated Fat: 1.4 g   **Trans. Fat:** 0 g

Cholesterol: 7 mg

Sodium: 99 mg

Potassium: 221 mg

Total Carbohydrates: 10.8 g

Dietary Fiber: 1 g   **Sugar:** 9.8 g

Protein: 30.8 g

Vitamin A: 5%   **Vitamin C:** 7%

Calcium: 14%   **Iron:** 3%

Ingredients:

- 1 1/2 cups peaches, frozen
- 6 ounces Greek yogurt
- 1 cup reduced- fat milk
- 4 pack gelatin
- 1 cup ice

Directions:

1. Put all of the ingredients into the blender. Blend until smooth.

Apricot Smoothie

This smoothie is easy to make and only requires 5 ingredients. It has the perfect amount of sweet-tart flavor and the whole milk and Greek yogurt enhances the yummy apricot flavor. The added protein makes this treat feel more like a meal.

Serves: 4
Prep. Time: 3 minutes
Blend Time: 2 minutes

<u>Nutritional Facts</u>

Serving Size: 248 g

Calories: 276
Total Fat: 9.3 g
Saturated Fat: 8.7 g   **Trans. Fat:** 0 g
Cholesterol: 3 mg
Sodium: 104 mg
Potassium: 311 mg
Total Carbohydrates: 11.1 g
Dietary Fiber: 1.1 g   **Sugar:** 10 g
Protein: 31.0 g
Vitamin A: 25%   **Vitamin C:** 11%
Calcium: 14%   **Iron:** 3%

Ingredients:

- 6 ounces Greek yogurt
- 1 cup whole milk
- 1 1/2 cups apricot
- 4 pack gelatin or 4 scoops isolate protein
- 1 cup ice

Directions :

2.   Put all of the ingredients into the blender. Blend until smooth.

****

Apricot Peachy Slush

When you want something cold to drink, nothing tastes better than an icy fruit smoothie! Try this mellow blend of peach and apricot for a refreshing drink that's high in Vitamin C.

Serves: 4

Prep. Time: 3 minutes

Blend Time: 2 minutes

Nutritional Facts

Serving Size: 270g

Calories: 42

Total Fat: 0.2 g

Saturated Fat: 0 g   **Trans. Fat:** 0 g

Cholesterol: 0 mg

Sodium: 5 mg

Potassium: 2143 mg

Total Carbohydrates: 10.4 g

Dietary Fiber: 1 g   **Sugar:** 4.2 g

Protein: 0.6 g

Vitamin A: 13%   **Vitamin C:** 44%

Calcium: 2%   **Iron:** 2%

Ingredients:

- 5 1/2 ounces apricot nectar
- 2 peaches
- 1 1/2 cups ice
- 1 tablespoon lemon juice
- 1 1/2 cups carbonated water

Directions :

      1.   Put all of the ingredients into the blender. Blend until smooth.

****

Conclusion

Thank you again for downloading this book. I hope that the recipes help you stay on the Ketogenic Diet!